CHIP FRENCH FRY'S ICKY, STICKY DIGESTIVE SYSTEM JOURNEY

by Jamee-Marie Edwards illustrated by Mariano Epelbaum

PICTURE WINDOW BOOKS
a capstone imprint

Hi there! I'm Chip. Life in my warm, salty fry box has been great.

But now, my world is being turned upside down. Where am I going?

Yikes! I'm heading into a place called the digestive system.

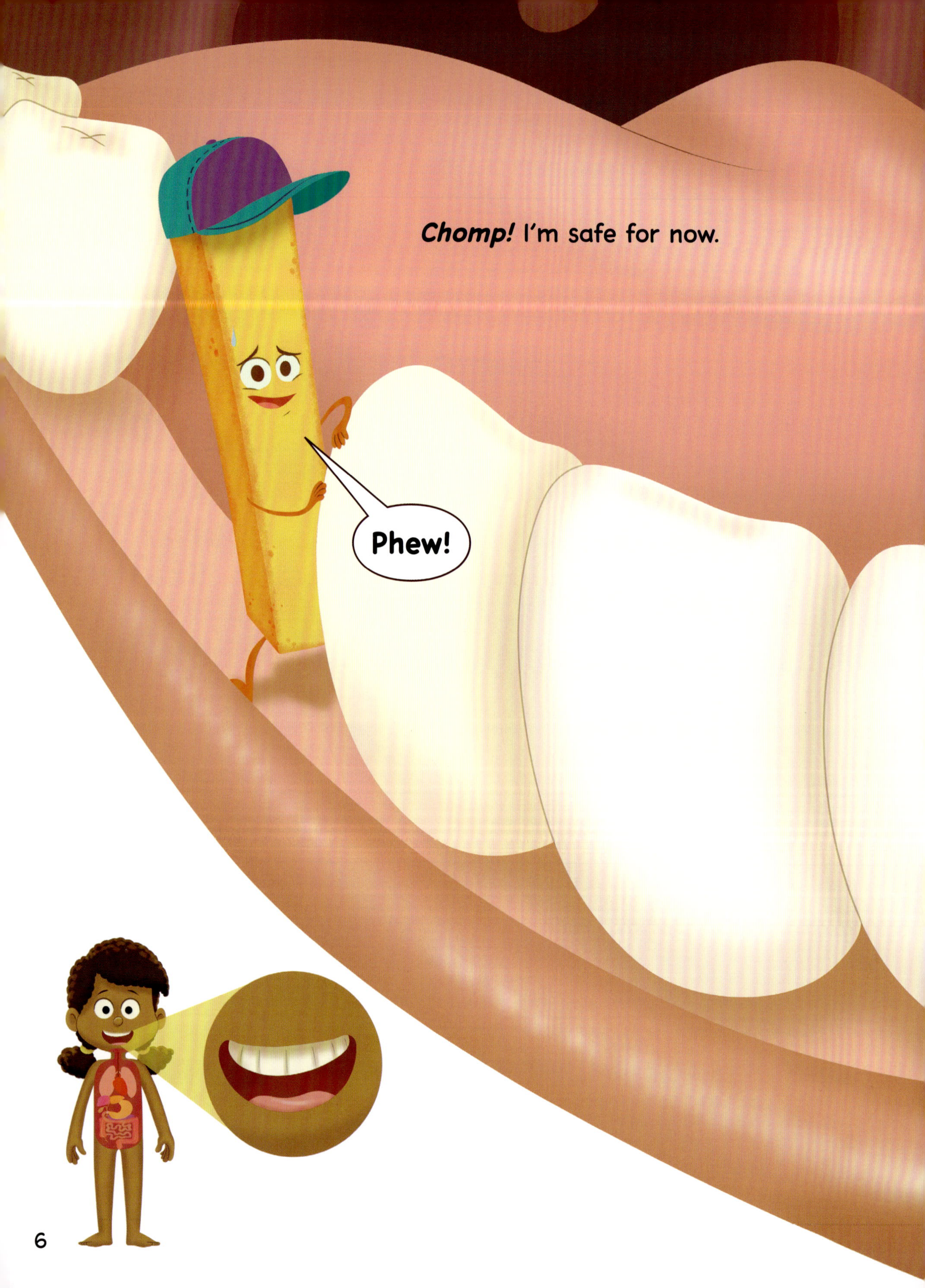
Chomp! I'm safe for now.
Phew!

YUCK! I'm getting covered in this goopy stuff called saliva. My crispy skin is turning mushy.

Saliva wets food. This makes food easier to swallow. Saliva also starts to break down some carbohydrates, like sugar in foods. Guess what? I'm made of carbohydrates!

Chomp! Teeth break down food into smaller pieces. Different types of teeth are in the mouth. Incisors cut food. Canines tear food. Molars grind food.

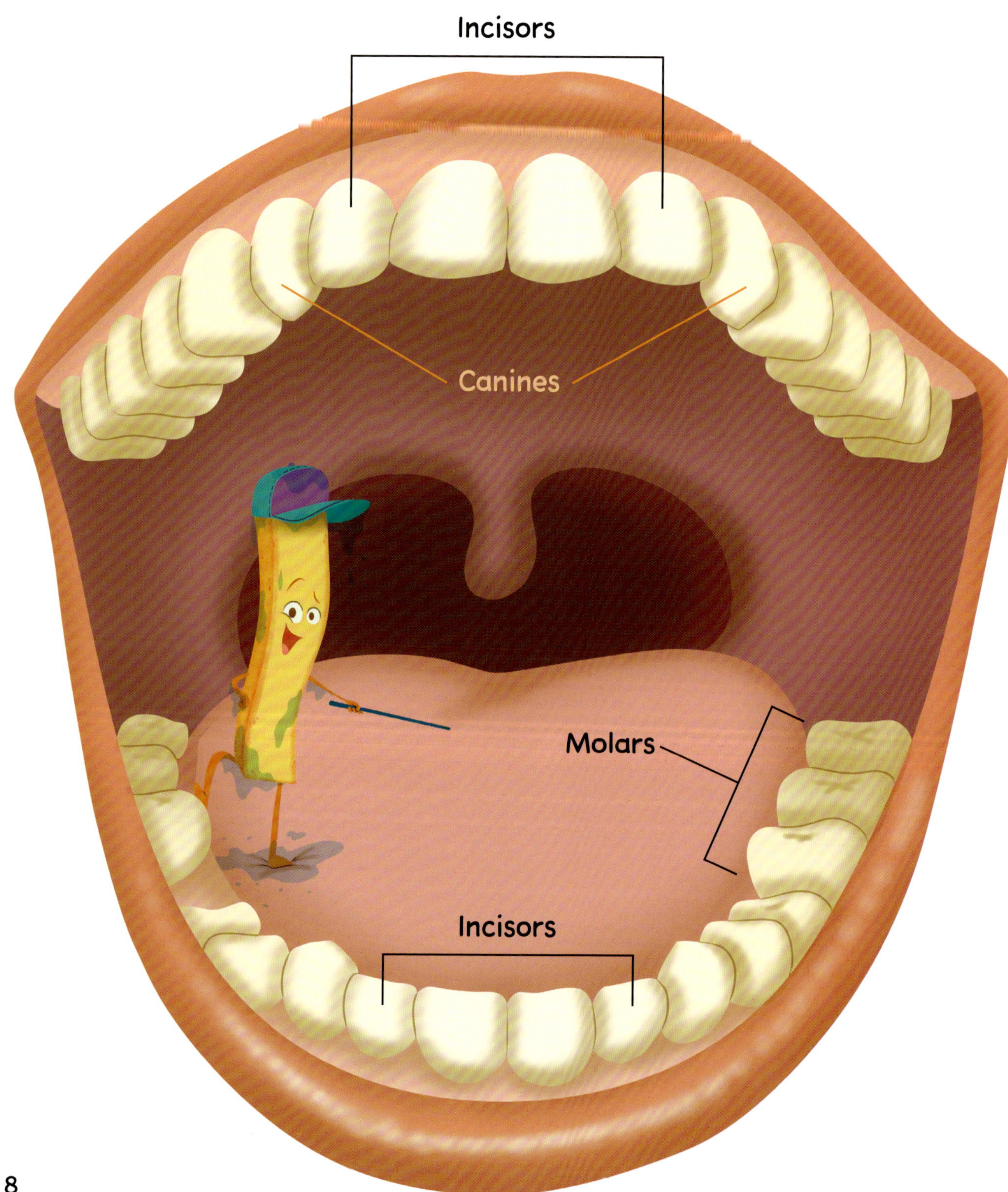

This is scary. I wish I was back in my fry box.

Chomp! Chomp! I'm really chewed up now.

A wet wiggly thing called the tongue drags me backward. It's pulling me toward a place called the throat.

It's dark in here.

Oh, by the way, the tongue has taste buds on it. Taste buds are tiny cells that let you experience different flavors. Yum!

Squish, squish, squeeze! Down I go into a stretchy pipe.

Muscles push me along. It feels like I'm being squeezed through a toothpaste tube. I'm in the esophagus now.

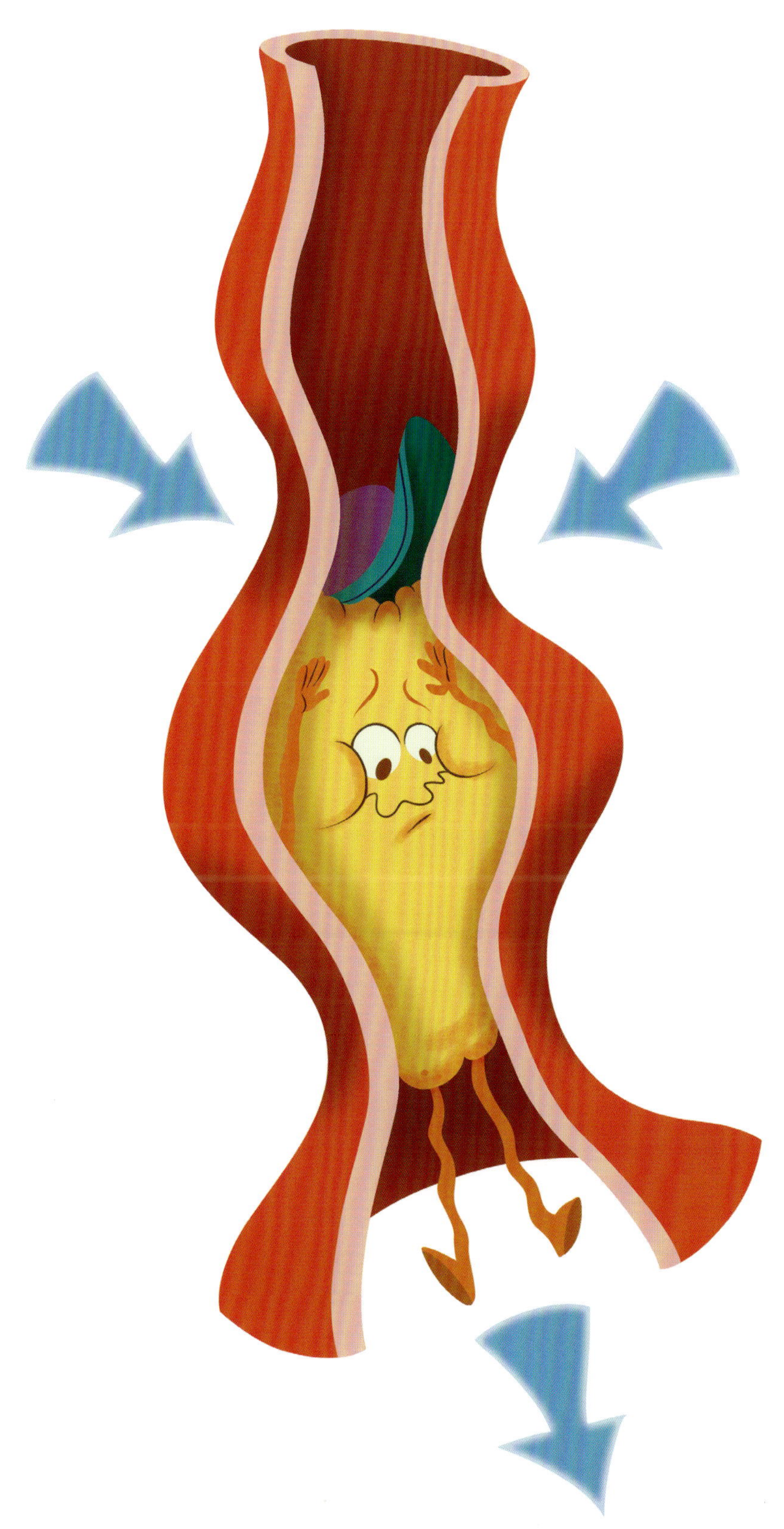

Seconds later, I'm in a stretchy **sac** called the stomach. It's shaped like the letter J.

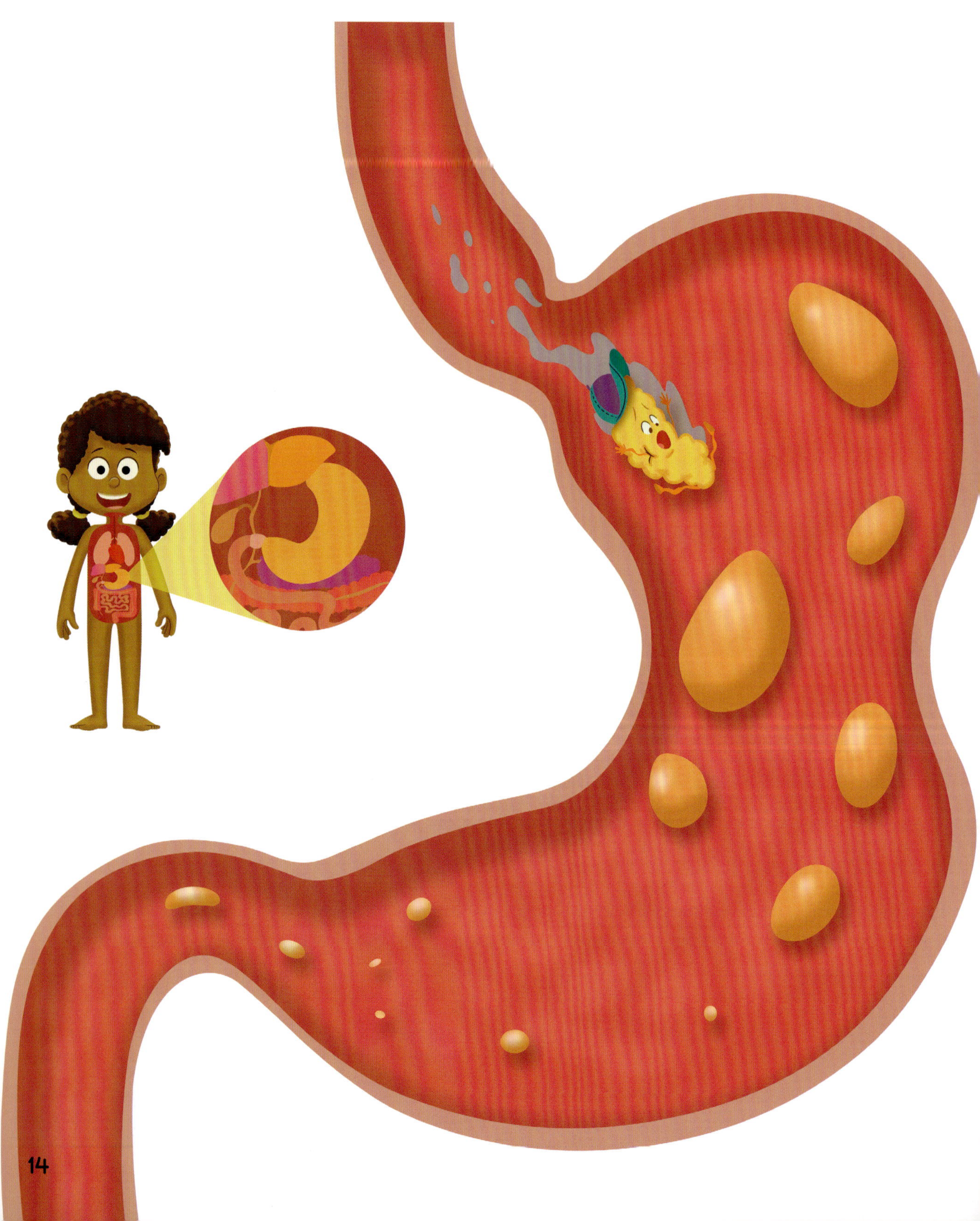

The stomach acts like a blender. I'm being mixed and mashed with other food pieces. My fry buddies from my box are here too! Muscles in the stomach help blend the food.

Being in the stomach feels like sitting in a bubbling pot of soup. The stomach is full of liquid called **gastric** juices that break down food. I am getting smaller and smaller. Gastric juices also help destroy germs in food.

Before leaving the stomach, I become a thick, mushy mix of undigested food and gastric juices. I look like vomit. Gross!

Around the bend I go into the small intestine. The bend is shaped like the letter C.

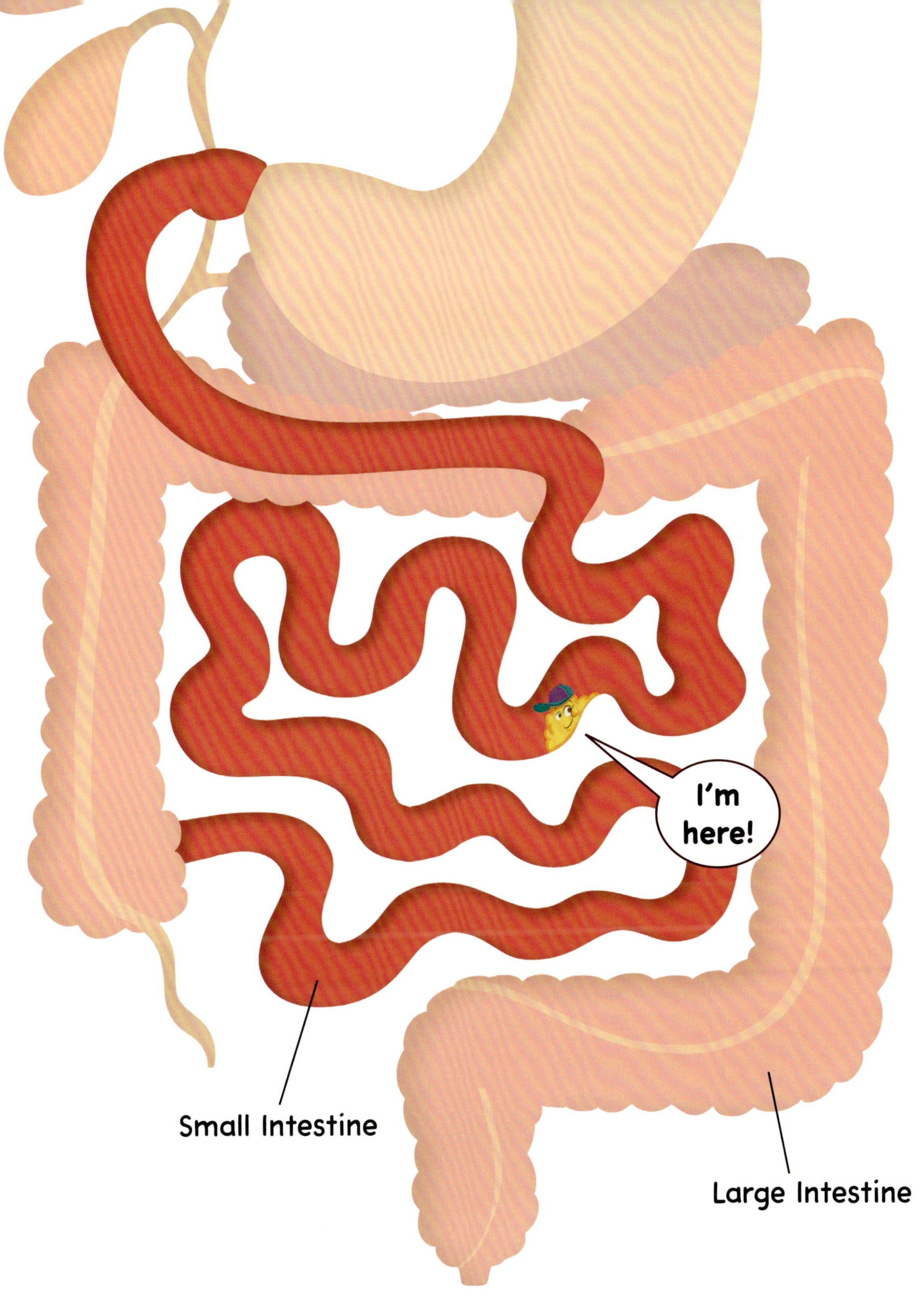

The small intestine is a long tube packed inside of you. The small intestine breaks down food into even smaller pieces.

The small intestine has three helpers. They are the pancreas, liver, and gallbladder. These organs connect to the small intestine with tubes called ducts.

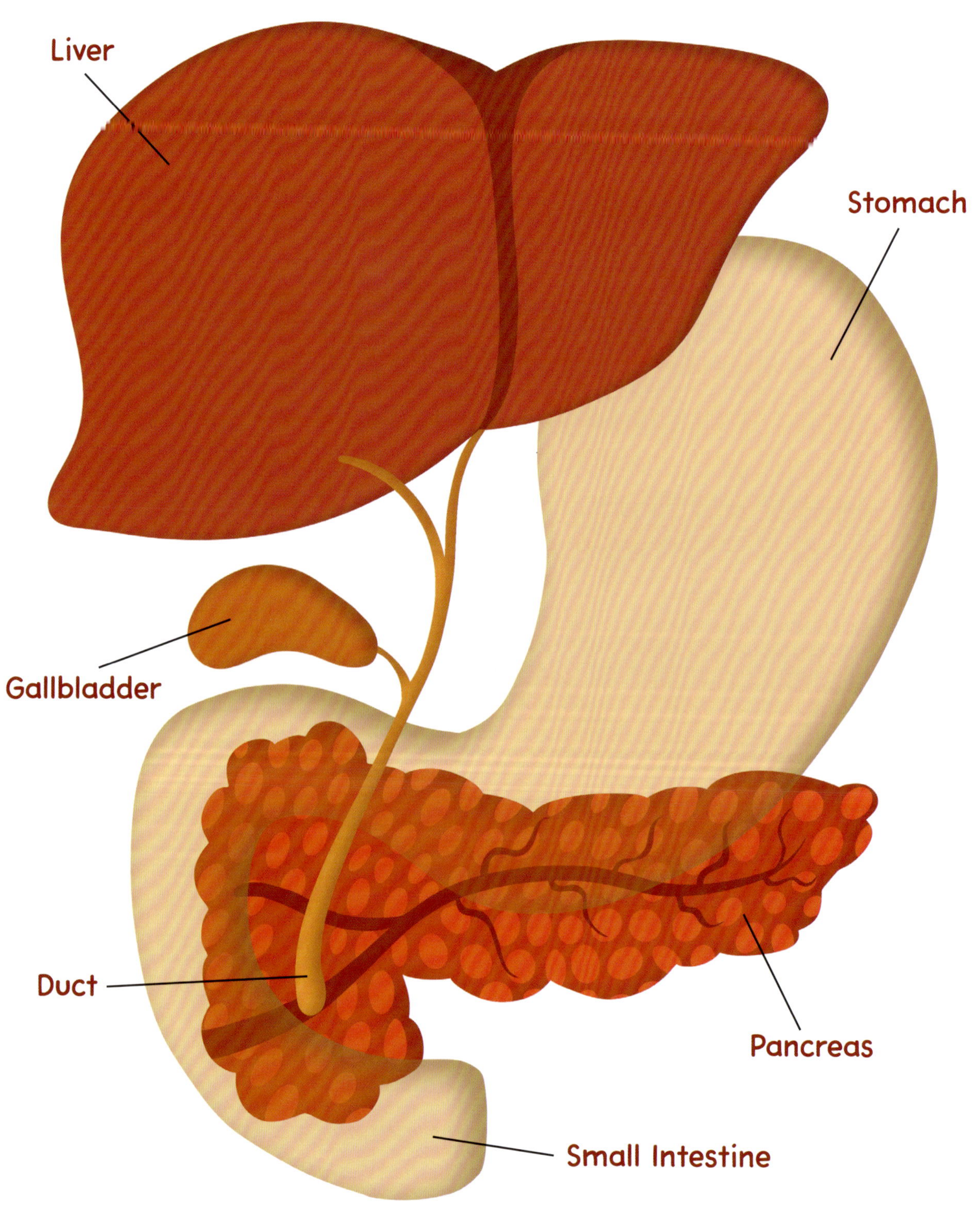

The three helpers work to digest food. The pancreas breaks down **proteins**. The liver makes bile. Bile breaks down **fats** found in food. The gallbladder stores bile until it's needed.

Bile looks like thick yellow-green goop. Ew!

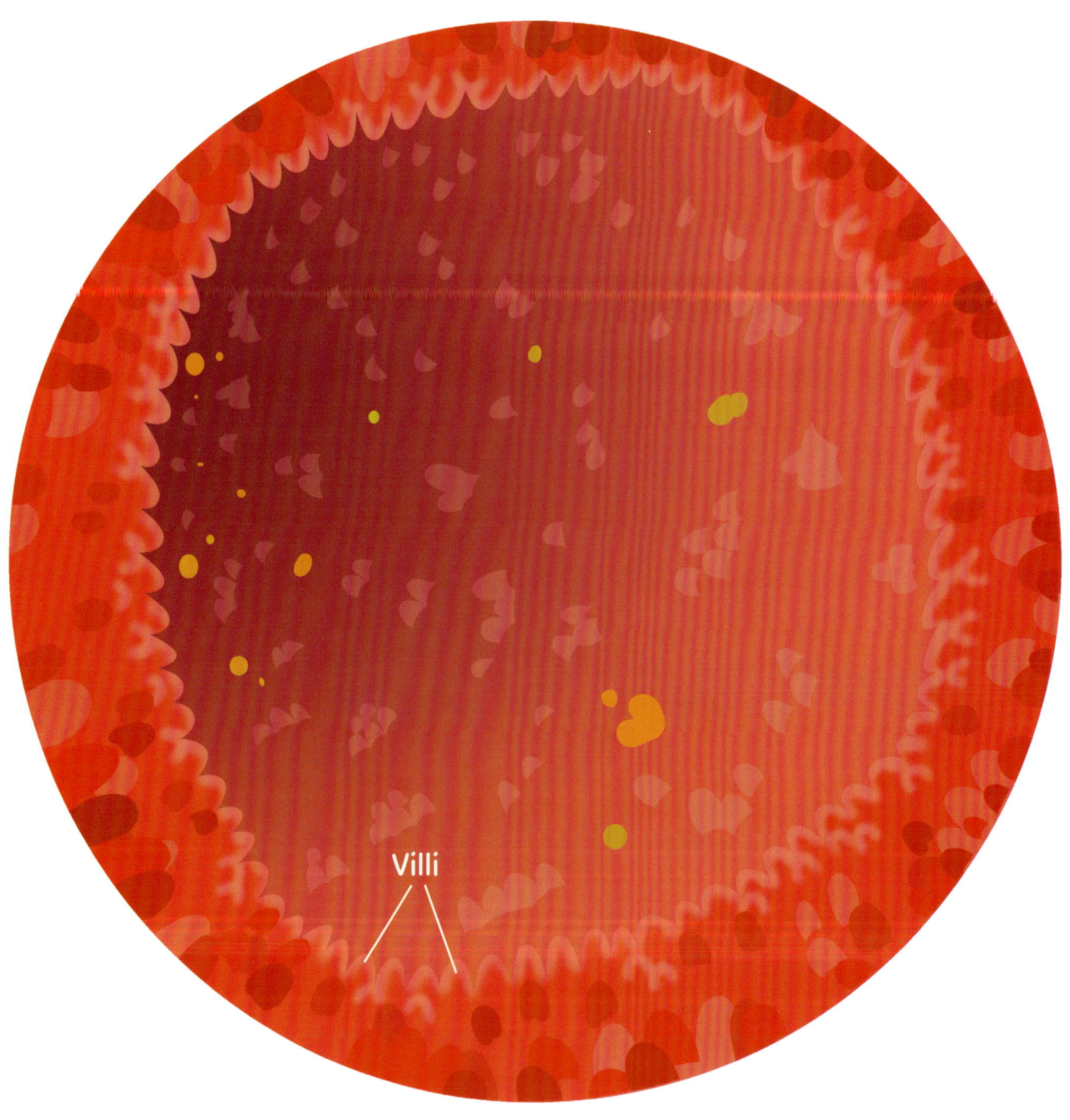

The inside of the small intestine is lined with tiny, finger-like shapes called villi. The villi help take in **nutrients**, like vitamins into your bloodstream. The blood then carries these nutrients to the rest of your body.

Nutrients give you energy to throw, jump, play, and think.

Next up is the large intestine.

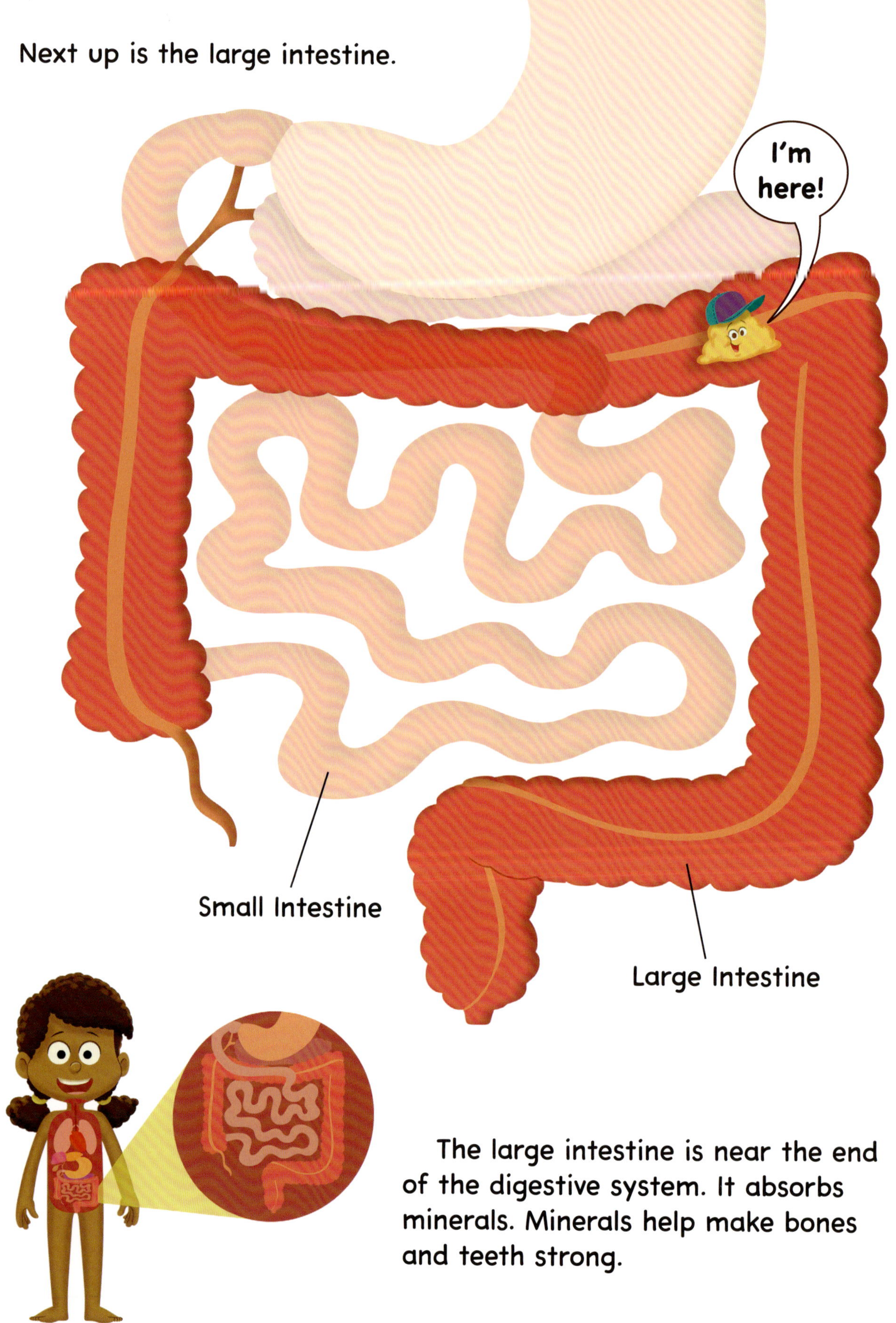

The large intestine is near the end of the digestive system. It absorbs minerals. Minerals help make bones and teeth strong.

The large intestine removes water from undigested food. Solid waste forms. It includes anything the body can't use. Solid waste leaves the body as poop.

Digestion is an important process. Your digestive system is like an engine that keeps you going. One bite at a time. Every time you eat, you're fueling your body. Let's review the journey!

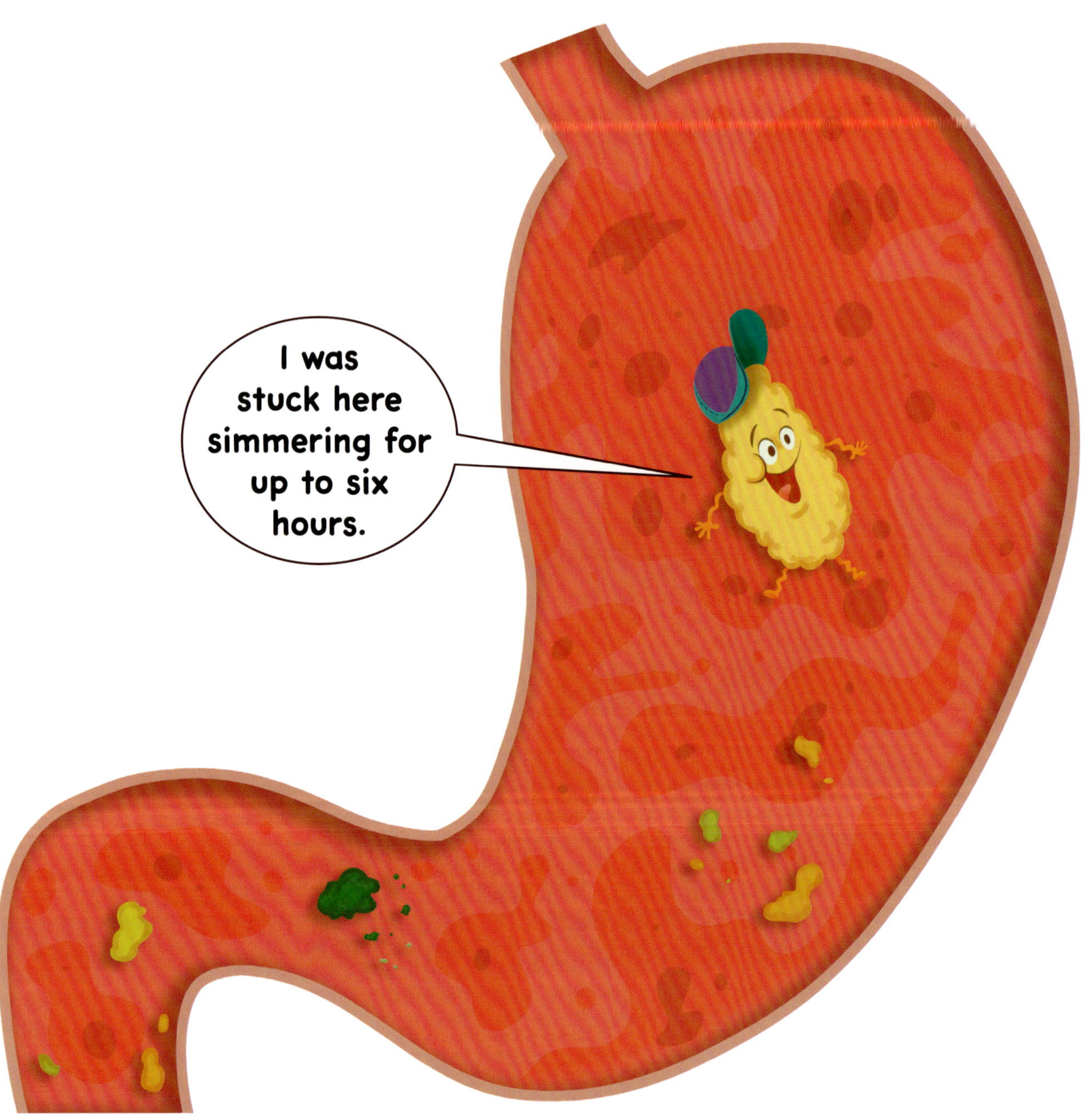

The trip through the digestive system can take anywhere between 10 and 73 hours.

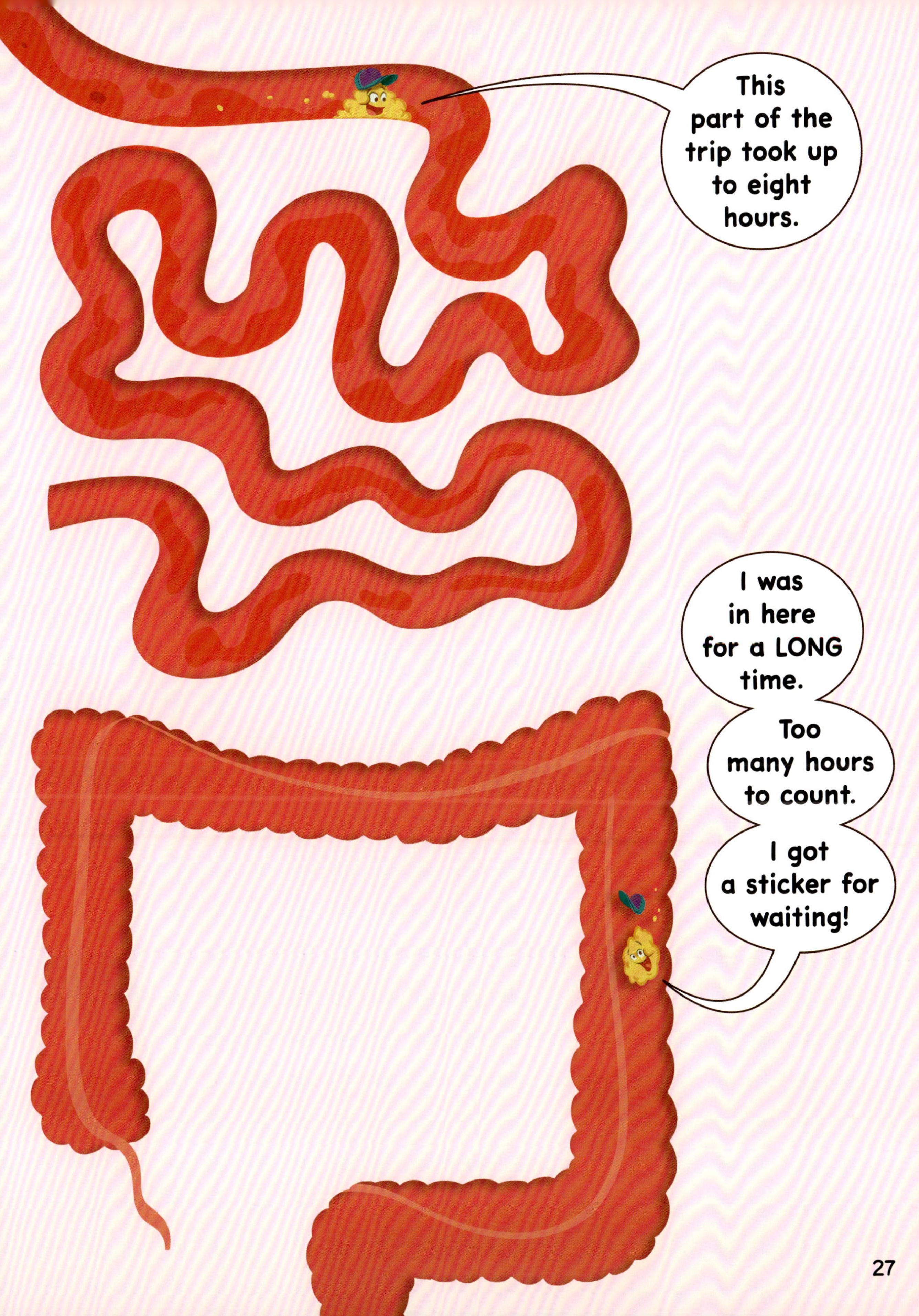
This part of the trip took up to eight hours.
I was in here for a LONG time.
Too many hours to count.
I got a sticker for waiting!

WHAT AN ADVENTURE!
CHiP
CHiP

Who knew going through the digestive system would be such a wild ride. I went through dips, twists, and turns. And places that seemed like endless tunnels. It was cool to learn that some body parts look like letters of the alphabet!

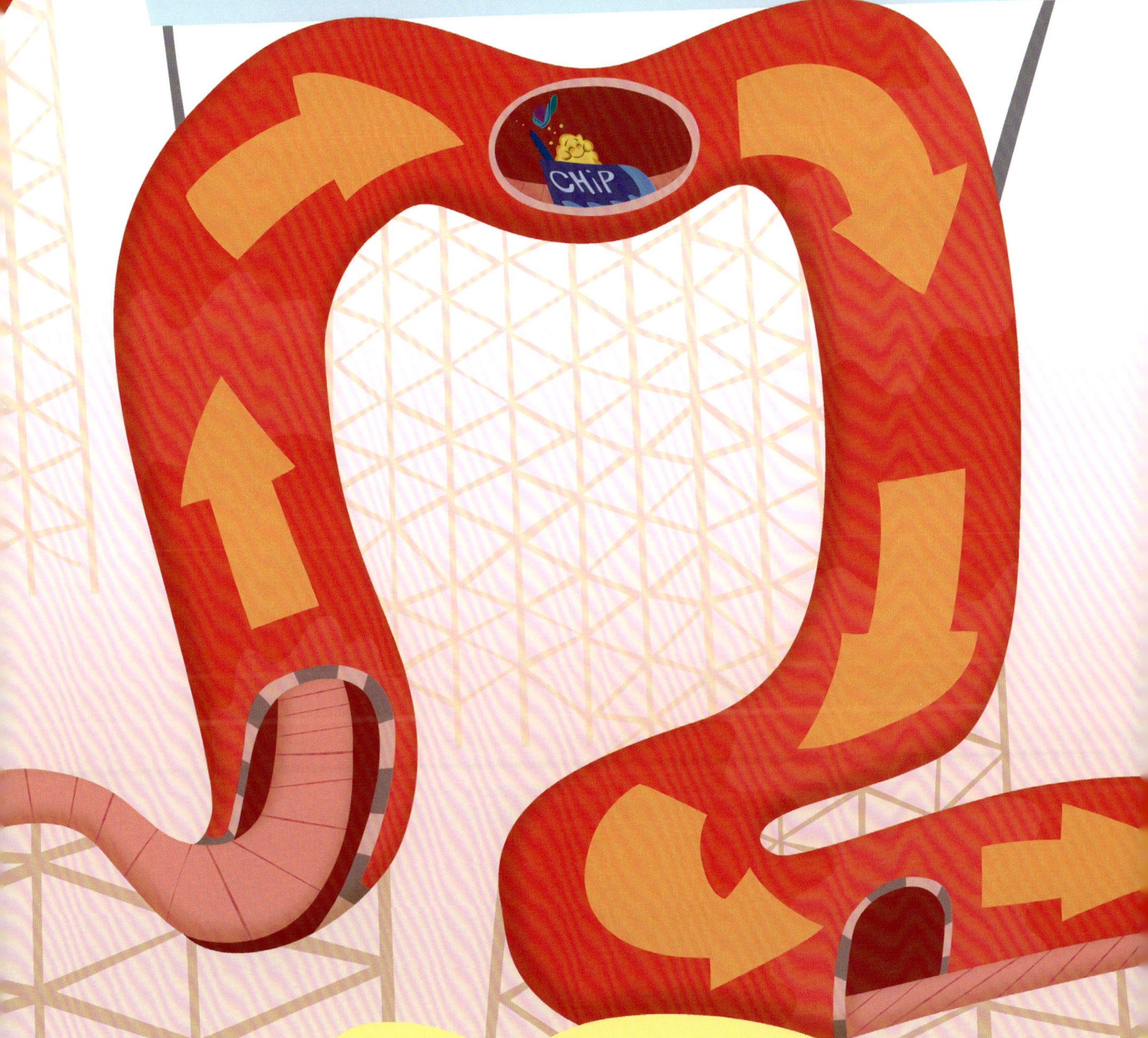

CHIP

Everything works together. Each part helps your body get the nutrients it needs to grow.

GLOSSARY

fat (FAT)—a nutrient found in food used by the body for energy

gastric (GASS-trik)—having to do with the stomach

nutrient (NOO-tree-uhnt)—a substance needed by a living thing to stay healthy

protein (PROH-teen)—an important nutrient that helps muscles grow; proteins are found in lots of foods like eggs, nuts, beans, fish, meat, and milk

sac (SAK)—a body part shaped like a bag or pocket

Photo Credit MaseFX

ABOUT THE AUTHOR

Jamee-Marie Edwards is an author, STEAM educator, and literacy advocate from New York City who is on a mission to ignite imagination and inspire children through creativity and education. Her experience in school health and health education has allowed her to connect with youth on various levels. As the founder of The Me I Need To Be Program, Jamee-Marie creates accessible platforms for learning in which she merges the Arts and Sciences to provide students with the opportunity to express themselves, build confidence, and gain essential skills. Learn more about Jamee-Marie at her website maeinspireu.com

ABOUT THE ILLUSTRATOR

Mariano Epelbaum is a character designer, illustrator, and traditional 2D animator. He has been working professionally since 1996 in various disciplines of animation and illustration, where character designs tend to be very expressive and original. Currently, Mariano works as an art director on several projects. He is always trying different styles and techniques.

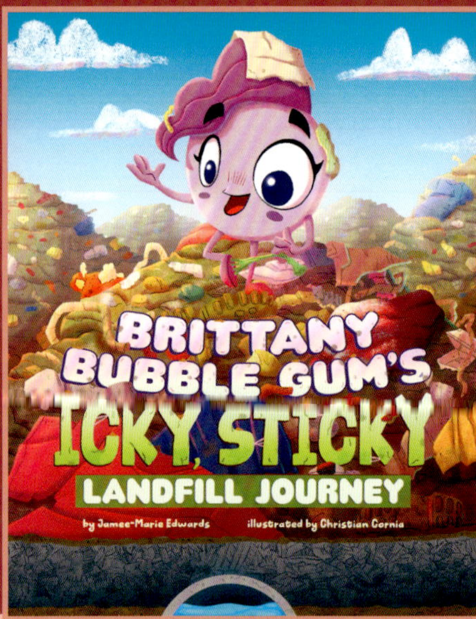

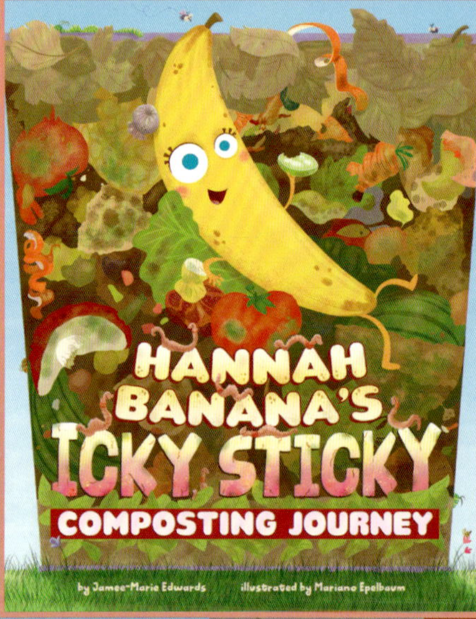

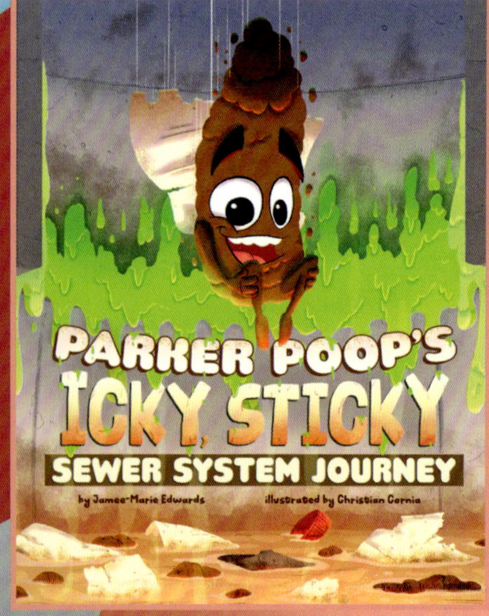

Published by Picture Window Books, an imprint of Capstone
1710 Roe Crest Drive, North Mankato, Minnesota 56003
capstonepub.com

Library of Congress Cataloging-in-Publication Data is available on the Library of Congress website.

ISBN: 9798875237935 (hardcover)
ISBN: 9798875237881 (paperback)
ISBN: 9798875237898 (ebook PDF)

Summary: An illustrated first-person narrative of Chip French Fry's journey through the digestive system.

Designer: Hilary Wacholz

Printed and bound in China. 006461